IMAGES
of England

NEWPORT,

CARISBROOKE AND PARKHURST

Newport Coat of Arms.

IMAGES
of England

NEWPORT,

CARISBROOKE AND PARKHURST

Compiled by
Phillip Blanchard

TEMPUS

Tempus Publishing Limited
The Mill, Brimscombe Port,
Stroud, Gloucestershire, GL5 2QG

ISBN 0 7524 2207 3

Typesetting and origination by
Tempus Publishing Limited
Printed in Great Britain by
Midway Colour Print, Wiltshire

38501. Newport, I.W., from the Air.

Newport from the air showing a large area from St George's Down to Blackhouse Quay and Fairlee to Watergate around 1931. The railways were being used to the full at this time, except for the Freshwater line which never made a profit. The quay was a thriving hub of industry and Shide Chalk Pit was still being excavated to feed the cement mills at Dodnor. At the time of writing, Newport is still expanding and now has a population of 18,864 inhabitants.

Contents

Harry Knight at the reins of his immaculate delivery horse and cart; waiting to be loaded outside Westmore's in Church Litten, Newport.

Acknowledgements

This book has been compiled largely from my personal archive of photographs, postcards and local information. However, without the help of my friends Dave Warne, Ken Fairweather, Maureen Grant and Mr and Mrs H. Crutcher for the loan and identification of some photographs, I would not have finished this publication. I would also like to thank Edna 'Thissey' Thistleton for her valued help with her family's history. I must also give thanks to all of the locals who have passed on snippets of information that I have hoarded in my memory over the years which has enabled me to bring this book together. I have heard humorous stories and bawdy stories which are unfortunately unprintable, unbelievable stories which I found to be true and ultimately the sad stories best left alone. I am indebted to them all for sharing their knowledge and experiences with me.

Most of all I thank my wife Caroline for her encouragement, input, checking and typing the manuscript. Also my daughter Victoria who has for many years had to put up with my fascination with the past.

Finally, I must apologize if I have missed out any source which I have inadvertently failed to mention.

Introduction

Newport and its surrounding districts, as I have tried to describe in the arrangement of photographs and accompanying captions, incorporates Horsebridge Hill to the north, Blackwater to the south, Bowcombe and Alvington to the west and Staplers to the east giving an area of about twelve square miles.

With so many very good books and publications written over the past two hundred years about the Isle of Wight and especially those about Newport, finding something new to say was very difficult. However, for the new readers of this type of publication I hope that the information gleaned from it is of use and for the regular readers something new might be found of interest.

The town of Newport has been in existence as an important trading centre since the twelfth century as the 'New Port' for Carisbrooke and the castle, however, the Medina river has been used for import and export since before the Roman times.

Situated at the navigable head of the river, Newport lies between the chalk downs of Shide and the clay of Gunville. Readers who attended the Priory Boys' School when it first opened will remember the clay that clung to their shoes and trousers in the winter and the cracks in the playing fields nearly big enough to fall into in the summer.

The natural clay in the area was put to good use for making tiles, bricks and pottery. Gunville Brick Yard was the largest of the clay pits dug out and since its demise has become a private pond for anglers. In the 1850s Jas Spickernell was the brick maker, then Horatio Dennett, Pritchetts and Sam Saunders of Saunders/Roe fame who made the now very collectable Carisbrooke Pottery as well as the *Gunville* stamped house bricks.

The enormous pit at Shide, now left to nature, was dug out first by hand and then by steam driven excavators, the chalk being removed by rail to the cement mills at Dodnor, and the finished product exported from there to the mainland by coasters. Further across St George's Down gravel has been excavated by Vectis Stone for over seventy years for use throughout the island. Another natural resource in the Newport area was the forest at Parkhurst which was originally a Royal Forest or Park, and was mentioned as a *Parco Regis* in the Domesday Book. Wood cut from the forest, mostly older oaks, was used for building the wooden ships of the British Navy and Merchant Fleet from the fifteenth to the nineteenth century. Progress and industry left the wooden ships behind, as they were replaced by steel. Trees were then cut for pit props to be used in the coal mines, and for wood required for the building industry. The area's natural resources over the centuries have provided employment to numerous men and women and due to this the living area of Newport has expanded.

Newport, being situated where it is, still has a good many old houses and buildings in and around Sea Street, Quay Street, Lugley Street and Crocker Street. Many have been sympathetically renovated and maintained to a high standard over the years. The history of the houses in this area dates back to the seventeenth century, but some can be dated much earlier, as lathe and plaster walls are still being uncovered. When walking in any of these earlier streets of the town don't just look in front of you, but up at the façades and the roofs of the houses to see how skilled the artisans were in the previous centuries. How will our new estate houses (including mine) compare?

Over the centuries it is known that many famous people have lived in or around Newport. They were either born here, chose to live here, or were employed here. Charles I in November 1647 thought he would be safe coming over to Carisbrooke Castle whilst he had his troubles with Parliament, but the castle became his prison for just over a year. He visited Newport Town regularly and stayed at the King James I Grammar School building on the corner of Lugley Street and Lower St James Street whilst the Treaty of Newport was being drafted; history tells us of his fate.

In 1759 General James Wolfe who defeated the French general, Montcalm, on the plains of Abraham in Canada causing Quebec, and thus Canada, to fall to the British, spent his last night in England at St Cross House before joining his ship in the Solent.

About fifty years later John Nash the famous architect best known for his town plans, Regency style of building and the use of stucco for façades, visited Newport whilst designing the elegant Town and Guild Hall which has the Market House underneath.

A year or two after this the young poet John Keats, while resident in Castle Road at Carisbrooke, wrote the epic poem *Endymion*. On his return from Japan in 1895 the renowned seismologist Professor John Milne lived and worked at Shide Hill House in St George's Lane, Shide, where he built an observatory in the house for the study of earthquakes world wide. Locals in the Shide area were quite surprised on first sight of his Japanese wife, dressed in her traditional costume, going about her daily business. During his time at Shide, Professor Milne had many distinguished visitors with an interest in seismology including royalty from home and abroad. He remained at Shide until his death in 1913, his premises are still standing but are now divided into private accommodation.

Amongst the many notables of the art world who visited or lived in the Newport area was the prominent Victorian artist, Miles Birket-Foster, who painted exquisite watercolour scenes around Carisbrooke, as did Henry Wimbush whose prolific works were reproduced in the early 1900s into coloured postcard views. Although not able to get the chance to paint or sketch in Newport, George Morland ended up in the Court House accused of being a French spy after he was seen drawing in Yarmouth Square. After suitable explanations were given by his landlord, Morland was released with a reprimand.

Another Victorian artist who visited and painted locally was Alfred Vickers whose fine works in oil of local scenery are eagerly sought after. Finally, and probably the least well known but arguably the best locally born painter, was Fanny Mary Minns, who lived in Terrace Road, Newport, and then Glen Cottage, Carisbrooke. Fanny was a private art teacher who produced many fine local views and like Wimbush reproduced them on coloured postcards. She exhibited works in the London galleries and her paintings are much admired and difficult to find.

As with most capital towns the outskirts of Newport has its share of prisons. Camphill, Albany, and Parkhurst are all situated off the Cowes Road and over the years have housed some of the most infamous prisoners in the country. Parkhurst started as a prison for children in 1838 and is constructed of bricks made from locally dug clay by the inmates. Having these prisons on our doorstep might not be approved of by some, however, over the years it has, and still does, create a large amount of local employment.

Over the years Newport has changed considerably, some would say for the better, some for the worst. There are those who will remember queuing outside of McKinley's in Upper Pyle Street with basin in hand waiting for it to be filled with faggots and peas and the taste of Westmore's doughnuts, Lower's pork pies, and Jolliffe's meat pies - not forgetting Jim Phillip's hotdogs from his stand. Although the little family businesses and shops have gone, they are by no means forgotten.

Phillip Blanchard
February 2001

One
Central Newport

Upper High Street, Newport, Isle of Wight.   158.

Looking down the High Street from the bottom of Carisbrooke Road is the shop of R.C. Gray the tent and blind maker who is still trading locally ninety years on. To the left are the premises of E.J. Wray and Sons, the baker and grocer and below that is Cole's the wet fish shop. The granite drinking trough in the middle of the road was sited in June 1910 as a memorial to the late Sir Barrington Simeon.

The Castlehold Baptist church was erected in 1812, at a cost of around £2,000 pounds. Due to the increasing acceptance of the Baptist faith the church was enlarged in 1872 and at that time would seat 570 people, it is still a very popular church today.

Only a few people are watching the soldiers marching down into the High Street and past the horse trough outside Wray's at the top of the town in 1913. This was a common occurrence whilst the barracks at Albany was in full occupancy.

Newport High Street opposite the Castle Inn public house. William Williams was the proprietor of the Banana House fruit and grocery store at No. 73 when this photograph was taken around 1920. Before 1930 he had gone into partnership with Whittington and the shop name changed to Whittinghton & William's greengrocer. Holyrood Hall, two doors lower down, was at this time the Plymouth Brethren meeting hall. The Castle Inn is the oldest standing public house in use in Newport and is still a thriving concern. The premises are dated prior to 1600 and there is a local rumour that a tunnel exists between The Castle Inn and Carisbrooke Castle, over a mile away and is supposed to date to when Charles I was imprisoned there. A map is in existence compiled by J. Aresti, dated 1840, which clearly shows some form of tunnel leading to the west but the edge of the map ends at the pound in West Street, as does the tunnel. In all probability the map shows, but does not mention, that this tunnel is the former bored out Elm Wood water pipes supplying 'fresh' water towards Castle Inn and beyond, and which were laid during the 1600s from the Carisbrooke end. Mill Street, as the name implies, leads down to the creameries which were built over the northern part of the Home Mill watermill, which used Lukely Stream as its power source.

Taken just after the Second World War, this photograph shows the post office on the North side of the High Street with Oscar Victor Mainstone opposite at No. 64. Mainstone's sold everything from pedal cycles to prams and dinky toys to dartboards, another branch was at Union Street, Ryde. The banner flying further down is advertising Murphy Radios outside Young's Electrical Shop

A quiet day in 1913 a little further down the High Street. At No. 108 Charles Alderslade was the picture maker and artists' materials dealer with George Oliver's Boot and Shoe shop displaying his wares outside No. 109. Next to that was Colson Bros. the upholster and house furnishers, who were later to have premises in Lugley Street.

The Ryde photographer F.N. Broderick photographed this scene around 1910, from the middle of the High Street next to the Queen Victoria Memorial looking down towards the town hall. Vehicular traffic was quiet on this fine day and every shop front on the north side of the street had its blind or canopy down protecting sales goods from the sun.

Taken in the early 1930s in the High Street below St James' Square with the clock tower of the town hall in the background. On the left is the Westminster Bank Ltd, Bateman the optician, Boot's the chemist with A.E. Harvey the baker further down. On the right is the stationer's shop of A.G. Bird, International Stores and the ironmongers of Mrs Hayles, shown here displaying the large padlock above the front door. Traffic at this time in the High Street travelled in both directions.

From an upstairs window of Edward Morris's furniture store and warehouse in Newport High Street this view look out to Lipton's the Tea and Grocery Merchant at No. 130 opposite and the adjoining premises of the drapers Burton's at No. 131-2. Both remained at these sites until well after the Second World War.

The bottom of the High Street around 1906 looking up towards the town hall. Gas lighting was evident on both sides of the street and was installed about fifteen years previously. On the left with an enamel Nestlé's milk sign on the wall is the narrow entrance to Sea Street. The properties on both sides of the road were owned by various members of the Dore family who were the grocers, sub-postmaster, and boot and shoe shop owners. Eventually all were knocked down and the County Hall extension built.

Newport town hall photographed at a time before the First World War when a police constable carried out point duty on the junction of the High Street, Holyrood Street, Quay Street, and the back of St Thomas' Square; which was at that time a road. The Vine and Eagle Tavern public houses stood on opposite sides of the High Street with Murdock the piano forte manufacturers adjacent. Mellia's grocery store can be made out on the right and Heals the grocer can be seen behind the advertising lamp of the Vine Inn.

An unusual view at the top of Upper St James' Street taken from an upstairs window of Nodehill School. The building shown on the right is part of the Board School, opposite is Ralph's fruit and vegetable shop, the retail outlet from their Watergate Road Nursery. J.E. Snellgrove's overhead display, advertises the firms decorating business and large retail premises.

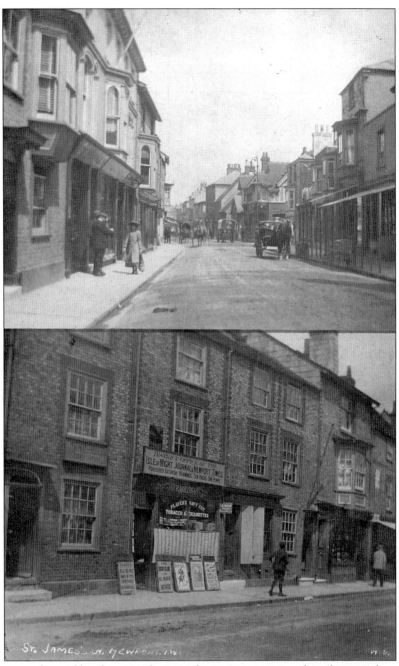

A few photographers of local postcards printed two views to a card, unfortunately many were rather dark and are nearly unidentifiable. However, the views from around 1910 of the top of St James' Street are unusual and worth looking at. The upper picture was taken from outside the Board School looking down towards the Plough Inn on the corner of Orchard Street. The lower picture is the shop front of Reynolds and Co. at No. 73 St James Street, who were not only a tobacconist, newsagent and sweet shop but the District Office for the *Isle of Wight Journal* and *Newport Times*. The newspaper was published on Saturday mornings, contained ten pages of local news and sold for one penny.

Newport Technical Schools.

The magnificent façade of the Technical School building, as it was known in 1910, incorporated the Secondary School and the Seeley Library, with the Board School just out of the picture further down Nodehill. Boys, girls and infants were all taught within the building which could hold over 800 pupils. The Seeley library later moved and the premises are now Nodehill Middle School. The county council purchased the site for this new building in the late 1890s but it was on Wednesday 23 July 1902, after the plans had been drawn up and accepted, that the two foundation stones were laid, in a civic ceremony, by Mrs Godfrey Baring and Miss Seely. The building was completed and occupied early in 1904 and immediately put to good use, not just in the daytime for children's schooling but in the evenings for adult education and lectures.

The market square was an exceptionally busy place not just for the buying and selling of animals but for socialising and gaining employment as seen here around 1920. Benjamin Vibert and Sons wine and grocery store can be seen behind Queen Victoria's Memorial. A few years after this photograph was taken Vibert's changed hands to become Weeks bakers and confectioners.

Looking across the animal market from an upstairs window of Home and Colonial can be seen the premises of J.H. Linnington who were ironmongers, gunmakers and agricultural implement agents. Tuffleys made breeches and The Lamb was a public house, a very thriving business due to its street corner location. All three firms are now gone, but not forgotten.

On Tuesdays and Saturdays the animal and corn market took place in St James' Square until towards the end of 1927 when it then moved to South Street, making the Square accessible to the bus companies seven days a week as a terminus. Seen here around 1925 are various buses belonging to the Vectis Bus Co., Dobsons, Enterprise and Colsons of Carisbrooke.

Queen Victoria's Memorial photographed from Timothy White's and Taylor's corner in 1905 with the Isle of Wight Club, or County Club as it was known, in the background. The County Club was built in 1810 of Swannage stone at a cost of £3,000. It contained a large and valuable library and newsroom and served the purpose of a social club for its wealthy members.

It was a common occurrence for one of the regimental bands who were stationed at the Albany Barracks, Parkhurst to give a concert in the market square at Newport for the benefit of the local people. This photograph is from a Thursday in early April 1906. From the cap badges it would appear that the bandsmen were men of the First Royal Fusiliers who were garrisoned on the island at this time.

A second view of the First Royal Fusiliers is from behind the band and looking into the gathered crowd at the foot of the Queen Victoria memorial. The photograph shows that Tuffley's lit up their shop front at night, with a fine set of three copper clad overhead gas lanterns.

Mr A. Hendicott, a local photographer, made this study of a group of local lads from the Isle of Wight Rifles Regiment at rest against the cattle railings in the market square in around 1910. J.R. Hayles the pork butcher and the National Provincial Bank can be seen in the background.

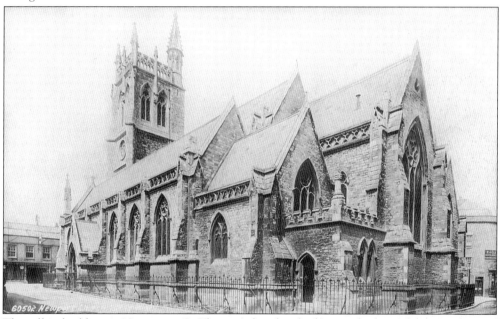

The tallest building in Newport is St Thomas' church, which was rebuilt on the original site of the ancient church, in 1854. It cost £20,000 to build, the funds raised mainly by subscription, bazaars and grants from the Church Building Societies. The foundation stone was laid on the 23 August 1854 by Albert the Prince Consort and the Grand Master of the Isle of Wight Freemasons. The church building was completed three years later and could seat 1,450 persons. Memorials, tombs and magnificent stained glass windows can still be seen and enjoyed to this day.

On Staplers Road at its junction with Cross Lane, in 1910 is the church of St Paul at Barton. Built in 1844 on donated land, the church cost £2,040 which was raised by subscription and grants. It is built from stone in the Norman style with a nave, chancel and small spire. When erected the church sat 400 people with half of these seats free for the local congregation.

This 1910 postcard shows the two millers' houses at Pan Mill with the pond in the foreground. Behind are the buildings in lower South Street or Cosham Street as it was originally known. Out of all the premises shown in the photograph, St Thomas' church on the skyline is the only one still standing.

Two

People, Politics and Processions

The unveiling, by Lt-Col. McKenzie Rogan, of the memorial plaques to the old boys of Newport Church of England Boys' School, West Street, Newport, who gave their lives for the country during the 1914-18 War. The ceremony was held in the presence of next of kin, widows, and relatives. The four gentlemen on the dais are from left to right: Mr King, a School Governor; Mr Chandler, the Headmaster; Mr Quinton, a School Governor; and Lt-Col. McKenzie Rogan, an old boy.

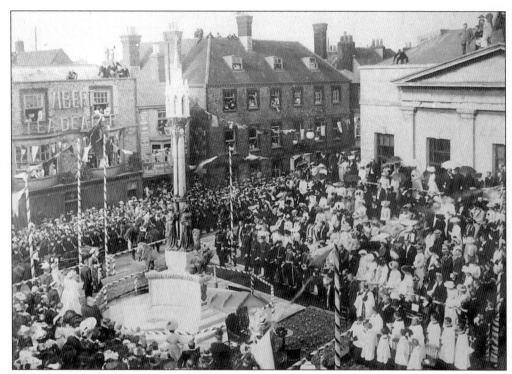

In August 1903 the memorial to Queen Victoria in St James' Square was unveiled by her daughter Princess Beatrice in front of a large gathering of invited guests and spectators. Every spare vantage point was taken up to view the spectacle including the roofs of all the surrounding buildings.

At the lower end of Staplers Road leading onto Snooks Hill are a contingent of officers from the Isle of Wight Constabulary leading a funeral cortège from St Paul's church, Barton along to Fairlee cemetery around 1930. Research is still going on regarding this funeral but it is known that the deceased officer was a Sgt Christopher Springer stationed at Newport.

The funeral took place on 3 March 1909 of the Mayor of Newport, Mr A. Gilmartin. The service was held in St Thomas' church, Newport. This photograph shows his coffin being placed on the horse drawn bier outside the church before being conveyed to Fairlee cemetery.

After the cortège left St Thomas' church the body of Mr A. Gilmartin was conveyed down Newport High Street towards Copping Bridge. The High Street was lined with mourners with the band of the Isle of Wight Rifles leading the procession; they can be seen here marching between the Eagle Tavern on the left and the Vine Inn on the right.

This view by local photographer H. Hollier is of electioneering in 1910 at the foot of the Queen Victoria memorial in St James' Square. This photograph shows the gathering crowd with mainly women waiting to get the best place around where the speaker will be. The notice board to the left is advertising a dog show taking place that day, unfortunately the date is indecipherable.

A further photograph by Mr Hollier shows Mr Douglas Hall, Conservative candidate, addressing a large gathering. The women are still in place but the majority of the assembly are male. During 1910 two parliamentary elections took place, both won by Mr Hall from the Liberals. The first, in January was an easy victory with a clear majority, but the December vote was won by the skin of his teeth, in just 300 votes.

The parliamentary election which took place in January 1910 was won by Mr Douglas Hall. This photograph by F.N. Broderick of Ryde is of Mr Hall arriving at Newport town hall with his entourage before the declaration of the vote being made.

With only newspapers and word of mouth as providers of information, public gatherings were a common event, especially at election times. The crowd seen here in January 1910 are leading down the High Street towards the town hall to await the poll declaration.

After the end of the First World War a further election took place on the 28 December 1918, again with Mr Douglas Hall being successful. Mr Hall and Mr Godfrey Baring are shown here on the balcony of the Town hall at Newport in front of the electorate on the declaration of the poll.

On the 6 May 1910 the reigning monarch King Edward VII died of pneumonia after being on the throne for a little over nine years following the death of his mother Queen Victoria. King George V took his oath as monarch on the following day. On Monday the 9 May 1910 the Mayor of Newport read out to the gathered crowd below the balcony of Newport town hall the proclamation that the country had a new King.

Three
Towards Parkhurst

The road to Parkhurst starts at Lower St James' Street below the market. For nearly one hundred years the Star Hotel or Inn had stood on the lower corner of Lugley Street, and by all accounts had a very good and thriving business. That was until a disastrous fire took hold on the 23 August 1910, thankfully no fatalities were reported but the premises were totally gutted. The Star never reopened and eventually the site was redeveloped and today it is a cycle shop.

During the many times that the circus came to Newport in the 1920s and 1930s the Town Gate mill pond became an elephants' bathing pool. In this photograph from the early 1930s, George Barton is on the horse nearest the camera with flat cap and moustache with, I am reliably informed, Neville Moses on the horse seated behind him. George and Neville escorted the animals from the circus site, which is believed to be at the back entrance of the old Newport football ground at Church Litten, to the mill pond at the bottom of Hunnyhill. Both men normally worked for Killeen's riding stables at Fairlee and also for the circus when in town. Circuses and fairs were an extremely popular form of summer entertainment especially between the war years. Wall's and Smitham's were the two main fairs visiting the island and supporting the carnival events throughout the various towns. As well as being urged to part with your money at the stalls, local motorcyclists were encouraged to have a go at riding their machines and defying gravity on the Wall of Death. More frightening and daring was the Globe, where the motorcyclists circumnavigated the inside of a huge metal globe with the momentum of the machine keeping the rider upside down. A local Shalfleet gent recalled riding the Globe in the 1930s. A few weeks ago Jack Barton, who is now well into his eighties recalled this event to the author and spoke of this feat as if it had only been yesterday. He even remembered what make of motorcycle he had ridden in this display.

This viaduct was built just prior to 1888, the date when the Newport to Freshwater Railway line opened. The viaduct structure has steel cross braces and uprights holding the bridge and all are supported on concrete pods laid on the mill pond bed.

Before and after the First World War a Soldiers Home and Institute was at the bottom of Hunnyhill by the bridge. It was capably run by Mrs John Roach the lady superintendent who lived at Westmill House, Carisbrooke. Soldiers of the many battalions stationed at Albany Barracks and the other batteries around the island could use the facilities or recuperate there after illness. The premises later became the Red Cross House and has only just moved to more modern premises due to redevelopment at Town Gate.

This view of Hunnyhill from 1907 shows not only the Blacksmith's premises of Frank Hawkins, but also the front of The Old Inn beer house with its upstairs bay window. The inn had a good local and passing trade with Albany Barracks being close by, but it shut it doors in 1916 no doubt due to the lack of trade as service men were posted overseas and also possibly due to the landlord being of dubious character. The premises are now private dwellings.

One of several blacksmiths shops in and around the town, this picture shows the premises of Frank Hawkins at No. 9 Hunnyhill, Newport around 1910. Apprentices are being supervised in the craft of shoeing horses. Mr Hawkins had been at the Smithy since late Victorian times but by the 1920s had vacated the premises.

The pony and trap is pictured outside of the Britannia public house at the top of Hunnyhill at the junction with Worsley Road. The photograph was taken prior to 1910 and it would be interesting to know if the little girl on the horse, whose face is glued to the unknown photographer, was the daughter of the landlord or a local child who lived nearby. With Hunnyhill being the main thoroughfare between Albany Barracks and the centre of Newport, it was not surprising to find that during the years that the barracks were occupied, there was a total of ten public, or beer, houses in the mile distance between the two places. Four were on the north side of the Town Gate Bridge. The first of which was The Old Inn, mentioned on p. 32, then The Britannia, The Halfway Inn, named after its location between the barracks and the town, and finally The Castle and Banner which had in the past been used as a gathering place for the local Albany Lodge of Freemasons. There were no licensed premises after this towards the barracks which was no doubt due to wise decisions taken by the licensing justices and the police. It must also be remembered that the close proximity of the workhouse nearby at Dodnor must have been taken into consideration. The remaining six premises between the bridge and the square were: The Trooper, just below Croker Street; The Lame Dog on the opposite corner; The Charles I, below the Black and White Grammar School; The Star Hotel (see p. 29); The Freemasons Tavern on the corner of Lugely Street, opposite; and finally, The Crown Inn, which was situated above Purkis's shop (see p. 64). Over the years recreation and social lifestyles changed dramatically, the barracks are long gone as has every single one of these public houses.

The Cooper family owned the post office and grocery shop at No. 38 Hunnyhill on the corner of Worsley Road from the late 1890s. This view from around 1920 with the children gathered on the forecourt has changed very little in the last eighty years.

The caption on this photograph from around 1920, states that this is Hunnyhill, Newport bu it is Worsley Road; which looks out over the fields towards Carisbrooke. Nothing striking abou this unusual view, the houses have not changed, but the road has been tarmacadamed sinc then.

Mr Montague R. Jones was the headmaster of Parkhurst Mixed School at Catherine Terrace, Hunnyhill on 4 February 1935 when this photograph of a display of handicraft also appeared. Amongst the work can be seen a pair of model garden swings, letter racks, and a cheese wire. The author has been unable to identify the eight pupils or even the class number, but if you can, the author would be pleased to know.

This group of ladies are celebrating Empire Day in 1913 in a house at the top of Hunnyhill between Catherine Terrace and the Castle and Banner public house.

Albany Barracks has been in existence since 1799 when it was first occupied by the Hampshire Militia. It was then host to numerous other mainland regiments over the years as well as the locally recruited Isle of Wight Rifles; which came into being in 1859 with six individual corps spread around the island. The following year they all joined together forming the Isle of Wight Volunteers and continued in different guises until finally being disbanded in 1967. This view from around 1910 shows part of the parade ground with several hundred soldiers all stood to attention.

The parade ground at Albany Barracks with an unknown regiment marching past the commanding officer who was taking the salute. The photographer, Mr Harry Hallier, is stood to his side and the author is certain that the dog leading the troops belongs to Mr Hallier as the animal turns up in numerous views taken by him.

The Royal Marine football team from 1905, judging by the globe and laurel cap badge, were stationed at Albany Barracks, Parkhurst. The military buildings can just be seen in the background disclosing the location's identity. Nearly fifty regimental teams from the Albany Barracks played locally either in the Isle of Wight leagues or friendly matches.

The barracks at Albany initially held 1,500 soldiers of all ranks. It was like a small self-contained town, everything a soldier required was supplied by the military, including food from the cook house, shown here.

The barracks also housed the married quarters for the service men as seen here. Recreational and sporting facilities were also provided as was a large military hospital with mortuary, and along Forest Road was the Parkhurst Military Cemetery. The revenue generated by the Army locally must have been considerable and sorely missed when the barracks finally closed.

Whilst Albany Barracks was in full use the Isle of Wight Fox Hounds met there on a regular basis. This photograph from around 1930 shows part of the hunt outside the officers' quarters awaiting the call to make off towards Parkhurst Forest.

Again from the 1930s with the officers' quarters in the background. Lady members of the Isle of Wight Hunt make off towards Parkhurst Forest and beyond for a day's sport.

Among the many regiments which were stationed at the Albany Barracks over the years were the Marines, who were billeted here at the beginning of 1907 at the time of this photograph. Bandsman Straw, on the left, sent this postcard to his relations after he had been drafted onto HMS *Exmouth* which was cruising with the Atlantic Fleet.

The main entrance to Parkhurst Prison in the 1920s showing the Isle of Wight Band waiting to be given entry through the great gates in order to perform a concert for the inmates. This was one of the many ways used by the prison authorities to help break the boredom and monotonous lives of the convicts.

A photograph by Head and Co. of 69 High Street, Newport, of the rarely seen frontage and iron gate of Parkhurst chapel situated on Horsebridge Hill below Noke Common Road. Like many smaller churches and chapels it fell into disrepair and has now been converted into a residential property.

Four

The River – Newport's Life Blood

aken from a large plate photograph, this vignette of the town of Newport is dominated by St
homas's church on the right with the River Medina flowing away in the distance and the Mew
angton Brewery to the left. In the foreground are the rear of the houses in Drake Road and the
nart fronts of the two and three-storey buildings in Terrace Road. The cement mills, in this
hotograph from around 1900, are on the west bank of the river.

This photograph, from around 1910, by Willsteed of Southampton shows a busy scene on the entrance to the quay. The chimney stack to the left belonged to the Electric Light Company and the crane mid-distance is loading a container of fruit onto a waiting flat bed cart, belonging to Caws and Co., to be towed around to their Lugley Street premises.

40972 NEWPORT: THE QUAY.

From the First World War, this photograph on Newport Quay looks downstream towards the Model Stores and its electric derrick at Little London. Huge amounts of timber are awaiting removal on the quayside where only one barge is fully visible.

Newport Quay photographed in the 1920s showing four of Croucher's vessels lying alongside the eastern wall and storage containers on the quayside. In the distance are the railway viaduct and the warehouses beyond in Sea Street.

With Fairlee cemetery and Hillside in the background, Crouchers sailing vessels fill the foreground of this photograph with one of their horse drawn delivery carts being loaded from the barge *Fox*.

On the quay can be seen a chain driven motor delivery van belonging to F. Prangnell o Newport. This rather faded photograph shows Newport Quay before 1920, where Shell Oil also had a depot. Mr Prangnell delivered Shell-Mex fuel and oils by contract around the Isle o Wight.

Crouchers had been operating from their Quay Street premises and from Newport Quay sinc the late Victorian times. The firm ran barges to and from Portsmouth and Southampton an also to other south coast ports delivering and returning with goods. This view is of one of th many vehicles owned by Crouchers and shows two of the delivery men who I am reliabl informed were Alf and Fred Grimes. The photograph was taken in the 1930s.

Another local photographer, A. Hendicott, photographed this Ford Model T light lorry which belonged to Harry Rolf and Sons of Staplers Road, Newport. Mr Rolf's firm were haulage and delivery contractors working out of the quay. Excavating works were also quite close to the quayside edge. This was for the electricity power lines, which were laid under the river bed near to the Model Stores, from the Newport Electric Light Works at Little London. The cables were brought by the shortest distance to the east side of Newport for commercial and domestic supply which was then replacing gas lighting.

66330. Newport, On the Medina, Isle of Wight.

Commercial sailing barges are seen at the entrance to Newport Quay in this photograph from around 1910. The barge in mid-stream fully laden with timber is being poled towards the quay and no doubt the owner is wishing for a quick turn round.

A group of H.W. Morey and Sons workmen are stood in front of the firms steam engine. This rather faded photograph looks across to the Model Stores on the opposite side of the river, with the immaculate steam engine and heavy trailer belonging to Morey's in the foreground.

The yard of the Newport Gas Works with the gas holder off to the left. Two sets of weighing scales can be seen in the picture, these were used for the sale of coke to anyone that purchased and took home their one hundred weight sacks. The reason for the photograph being taken was to show the fire smouldering in amongst the tons of coke in the tip.

This group of employees from the Newport Gas Works are posed beneath one of the railway viaduct arches. Nearly all are sporting buttonholes and one man standing in the centre is carrying a bugle, at the time of publishing the reason for the photograph being taken is unknown, if any reader knows the reason why the author would be pleased to know.

Along with W.H. Morey and Son, Alexander Sharp and Co. Ltd were the main merchants and importers of timber on the Island. Like Morey's they were able to carry out machining of all woods in their workshops. This photograph from around 1910 shows a group of workers in the wood store on the quay at Newport.

The yard of Alexander Sharp and Co. Ltd on Newport Quay showing a group of hardworking individuals posing for the camera. Waistcoats were the order of the day at the time of this photograph, around 1920.

Five

Business and Commerce

This photograph from around 1910 shows part of Elm Grove looking in the Carisbrooke direction. Built in the mid-nineteenth century, the terrace of houses is still there virtually unchanged, except for the grocery shop with the lower bay window which is displaying goods. The upper bay window was above the entrance to the same premises but this was into the small beer house called *The Gardeners Rest*. This closed in 1970 and became a private dwelling.

This photograph from around 1907 shows West Street from the Trafalgar Road end and also Morey's Wood Yard on the left. In the far distance are the shops on the corner of Drill Hall Road and Carisbrooke Road.

William Henry Morey and Sons of West Street, Newport had a timber yard in Trafalgar Road and Albion Steam saw mills in Terrace road. The firm dates from the 1860s and since that time as well as using local and mainland timber, imported the finest woods from throughout the world. This 1908 photograph shows the inside of the saw mill in Terrace Road. As well as being the owner of the wood yard Mr Morey amongst other things was a director of Messers. Pritchett and Co. Brick, Tile, Pottery and Terracotta Manufactures at Carisbrooke.

Westminster Lane was somewhat different than it is today at the time of this photograph in 1904. The rear of the houses in Caesar's Road can been seen with their gardens running down to the expansive pond of Westminster Mill which was at that time a working mill. The chimney to the right was to exhaust the smoke gases away from the supplementary engine which was used in a addition to the water driven wheel.

20, S^T JAMES' SQUARE, NEWPORT.

AUCTIONEER WADHAM UPHOLSTERER

HEAD ESTABLISHMENT.

A nineteenth-century engraving showing the premises of C.H. Wadham of No. 20 St James's Square, Newport. Spread over four floors with entrances in both the square and the High Street, the shop was immense and stocked everything for the home.
Established in the 1860s it remained one of the prestigious retailers in Newport until its closure. Wadham's also made their own furniture and had workshops for repairs, re-upholstery and French polishing.

Now long gone, the shop of Frederick H. Bevis at No. 52 High Street, Newport not only sold flowers and fruit but was a supplier of shrubs, trees, wreaths and floral displays. Mr Bevis owned another shop at No. 100 St James's Street and judging by the worn front step shown in the photograph must have had a successful business.

The premises of Archibald G. Bird, stationery and bookshop, at No. 43 High Street, Newport. This shop front display photograph from December 1927 and was featured in *The British Stationer* magazine the following March where it was praised for its decorative content. Mr Bird opened the shop in the early 1900s and with the valued help of the manager Mr Lorenzo Bennington continued until both were well past their retirement age.

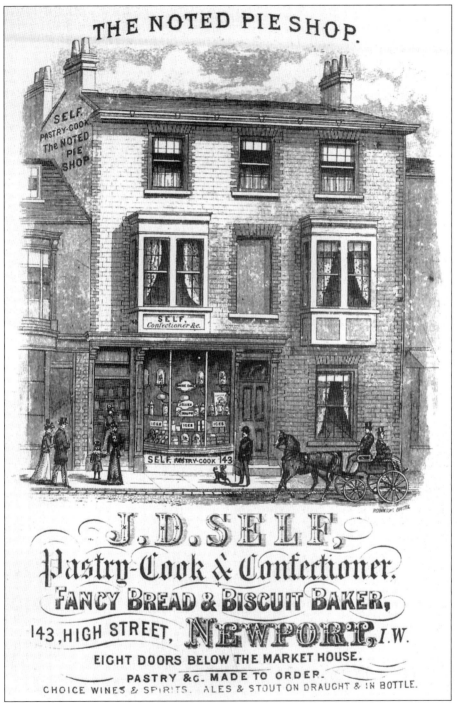

An engraving of the premises of John Dawson Self of No. 141 High Street, Newport. A self explanatory print informing the new customer of its location and goods. Mr Self traded in the late 1800s up to just after the end of the First World War when Bertie Jolliffe took over the bakery and shop.

The premises of Albert Milton Cheverton, taken by local Newport photographer Ernest A. Kime, were situated just below the town hall in the lower High Street. This display of motorcycles from 1908 shows consecutively numbered Isle of Wight registered DL machines. The shop sold everything from nuts and bolts and perambulators to pedal cycles, new motorcycles and sidecars. Mr Cheverton started his business in the late 1890s here in the High Street and as modes of transport progressed so did his business. By the early 1920s his cycle shop had moved to 112 Lower St James Street with Stanley Russell taking over at 138 High Street and Witham Bros. moving into 139 as a cycle agent and motor engineers. Within just a few years this was gone and replaced by the locally renowned Medina Café and confectioners with Mr Cheverton still trading as a pedal cycle dealer on the opposite side of the street from where he started. Now, like most shops in the High Street 138/139 has changed and is now an estate agent, the frontage has been altered but the upper floors remain the same.

Owned by Mew, Langton and Co. Ltd, The Cranbourn public house is situated on the corner of Trafalgar Road and Upper James's Street. This photograph shows the street dressed in banners and bunting in May 1937 for the Coronation of King George VI and Queen Elizabeth.

Taken in 1904 this photograph is of the staff of Albert Edward King whose shop was at No. 79 St James's Street known locally as Node Hill. The business made and sold new and used furniture on the premises. This picture is from outside of the rear entrance which was in Trafalgar Lane which ran between Chapel Street and Trafalgar Road.

A young Alfred George Riley is shown stood in the entrance to his hairdressing premises at No. 82, St James's Street in around 1910, he later owned another hairdressing shop in the High Street, Newport. On the upper floor next door at No. 83 was a registry office for servants wishing to seek or change employment, no doubt a private forerunner of a Job Centre. On the ground floor was the shop belonging to Miss Nellie Tuffley which was a fancy repository.

This bay-windowed bakers shop, from around 1910, was located at No. 80 Upper St James's Street and was owned and run by Mrs Ann Cave. She had been there during the latter years of Queen Victoria's reign and was eventually joined by another baker to become known and trade as Cave and Williams in the early 1920s.

An advertising photograph of the shop front and display of the wholesale grocers Upward and Rich situated at Nos 50-51 Pyle Street in around 1930, this ran through and backed on to South Street where the wholesale goods were stored and deliveries loaded. The Upward's firm were in existence for over two hundred and fifty years before ceasing to trade.

This photograph from around 1920 is of Miss Angelica Colson in the doorway of her small grocery and confectionery shop at No. 87 Pyle Street, Newport. She was related to the furniture dealer by the same name who had premises in Lugley Street at this time. Looking at the many sweet jars and tins on display, this shop must have been heaven to children with a halfpenny in their pockets.

This photograph from 1904 shows Daish and Co. the outfitters at No. 116 Pyle Street, Newport. The firm had moved from St James's Square a couple of years earlier and was run by Louis and Harold Daish. The shop later became suppliers of clothes to the Scouting movement under the guidance of the owner 'Sam' Daish.

St Thomas's Square at its junction with Pyle Street shows The Wheatsheaf Inn with the family name of the licensee J. Read above the door. In existence since the mid-seventeenth century, the inn has been extended over the years and is still a busy hotel today. This photograph from 1920 also shows Daish and Co. with its sun blinds drawn protecting the clothing in the window from the mid-day sun.

This photograph from 1907 shows the premises of William Dukes at No. 4 St Thomas's Square, Newport. Not only was Mr Dukes a gas and hot water engineer he was also a turncock and tinsmith. The shop front has changed very little over the years but it has expanded. The lady standing holding the cat in the doorway was Mrs Heard the housekeeper to Mr Dukes.

Thomas Bowler is shown outside of his shop at No. 9 St Thomas's Square, which was situated behind the church. Mr Bowler was a pawnbroker at these premises for a considerable number of years during the early part of the 1900s. On p.88 is a distant photograph of the front of his shop with the three balls of his trade sign suspended from the front wall on an upper floor.

This 1930s rear view of Gods Providence House shown from Town Lane has not altered in over sixty years. The street lamps have converted from gas to electric, and the Wadham's advertising sign has gone with the firm, although part of it can just be seen today. The car parking area is now used only for motorcycles. The church and town buildings are still there and the restaurant is still a thriving concern.

Lower Pyle Street, opposite what is now the Dower House Medical Centre, was the premises at No. 127 of Thomas and Co. later to become Thomas, Gater and Bradfield and Co. They were corn millers who owned and worked Pan Mill, Home Mill which was built on and is now the Unigate Dairies in Mill Street, and also above it on the Lukely stream the Westminster Mill. The premises at No. 127 Pyle Street was a large building used for the storage of corn, flour and straw.

Caws and James of No. 44 Lugley Street, Newport were wholesale fruit and vegetable merchants who supplied the whole of the Isle of Wight. This photograph from around 1910 shows off the magnificent fleet of delivery horses and carts along with Caws and James' staff. They later moved to larger premises further down at No. 55 Lugley Street.

In this photograph from around 1920 Caws have now become Caws and Co. and moved to No. 55 Lugley Street on the corner of Chain Lane. They have now become motorised and the advertising on the motor vehicle and the walls of the premises shows that they supplied everything for the grocer and greengrocer.

This scene is of the yard of Edward Munden in Lugley Street, Newport from 1908. The front of the shop was at No. 128 High Street which Mr Munden had acquired the previous year from Mr E.H. Harvey. Mr Munden was both a retail and wholesale provisions merchant making full use of the huge expanse of the premises that he owned between the two streets. The firm supplied all parts of the island and for the more inaccessible districts employed two mules in addition to the horse drawn carts

In 1927 the Cattle Market moved from its location in St James's Square to this new site which is now the Safeway's supermarket development. Entrances were in Church Litten between Westmore's and Dibbens the builders merchants and also under the archway seen in the photograph through into South Street. The buildings either side of the archway were formerly the Corn Exchange and Market Offices.

A posed photograph of just a few of the workers at W.B. Mew Langton Brewery in Crocker Street, Newport. Although a physically demanding job the young men are smartly dressed, mostly with collar and ties.

The building and construction firm of George Fielder Quinton of No. 1 Carisbrooke Road, were awarded the contract of sewer laying around Newport. This scene from around 1920 shows Mr Quinton in flat cap stood by his horse and trap overseeing the work being carried out in Staplers Road near to Polars, the home of the Mew family, the local brewers.

This view is of the shop belonging to Richard Bird Cheverton and Co. Ltd. at No. 50 Lugley Street, Newport from around 1910 displaying their saddles and tack. Mr Cheverton was also a coach and carriage builder with other premises in Lugley Street and Lower St James's Street.

George Barnard Purkis had owned a shop at No. 111 Lower St James's Street, Newport since before 1880 and acquired the premises next door a few years before this photograph of him and a member of staff in around 1905. Mr Purkis sold cheap durable boots and shoes and also ready-made jackets and trousers. Hanging up on the display amongst the hob nailed boots can be seen gaiters and spats.

Six

Carnivals and Shows

The Newport King and Carnival Queen are being escorted across the old Newport Football Club pitch at Church Litten on the 20 August 1930. The Pearly King is Ted Fairweather of Royal Exchange, Newport who was well known across the island as this character. The 'royal couple' are on their way to take their seats in the grandstand before watching the parade and field events.

This trade entry in the Newport Carnival from around 1930 is a lorry belonging to Shell-Mex Ltd Fuel and Lubricating Oil Co. who had premises on the quay. On the rear of the lorry are two people wearing large heads which were popular at carnivals on the island until the end of the 1950s, there is also a little girl dressed up as a clown. The photograph was taken in West Street just in from Carisbrooke Road. The Raleigh Cycles enamel sign was situated on this wall for many years after this event.

The same Shell-Mex Thorneycroft lorry, but this time photographed outside the Primitive Methodist church in Pyle Street, which is now the Salvation Army Citadel. The lorry has had its solid tyre wheels dressed with bunting as are the front axle and headlights.

The carnival used to line up in Church Litten and down South Street towards Furlongs due to the amount of entries. This coach and four in hand were entered into the event on the 23 August 1934 and stood outside of the Mission Hall in South Street with the Corn Exchange in the background.

Carnival day in Newport was on Thursday 20 August 1936, and this trailer exhibit was just one of the many topical floats, with the caricature of Mrs Grundy from the play *Speed the Plough* by Thomas Morton still going strong and even though three years before it happened the Second World War must have been in peoples' minds as shown by the placard on the cage.

This was Newport's last carnival before the outbreak of the Second World War. From this carnival came this beautiful horse drawn Queens Tableau shown here on Thursday 24 August 1939. Opposite and outside the *Dolls House* in South Street is an Isle of Wight Creameries van with advertising on the side and in front of that is a pony drawn creameries milk cart.

Shown from the rear garden of No. 26 Holyrood Street, Newport from around 1930 is a publicity entry for the Children's Carnival. The pedal car is decorated as a delivery van advertising the premises of Lily Way of the Vectis Café who was a confectioner at that address. The children are dressed as bakers with their bread delivery baskets, but the identity of the person in the centre is unknown.

o find a cart loaded with hay, drawn by two goats accompanied by two children at the bottom
f Quay Street would normally be most unusual, but these were entries in the Newport Carnival
round 1925 and were waiting for the procession to start off up towards the High Street. In the
ackground can be seen The Dolphin public house and the Railway Viaduct spanning the River
1edina.

1e afternoon Children's Carnival Procession lined up at the bottom of Quay Street around
^20, while one of the staff from Croucher's Warehouses in Sea Street is watching the assembly
>m the background. Always topical, the entries shown are 'gathering in the harvest' along
th the little boy on a tricycle. The first fire engine bears a Borough of Newport insignia,
1ilst the second engine shows a placard stating 'wake up Newport'.

The pedal car entry into the Children's Carnival around 1930 is prettily dressed up as a wishing well, complete with handle and bucket. The days taken to make this entry must have been incredible, with just crêpe paper and glue – no super glue, sellotape or bluetack available then. Behind this entry is a mobile amplifier van called the Singing Bus which was sponsored by *The Daily Express* newspaper. The photograph was taken at the old Newport football ground at Church Litten.

This little lad's pedal car entry No. 339 from August 1932 was in the procession which must have lasted a considerable time after parading around the town and ending up at Church Litten. In the background are Pan Mill and Staplers, whilst in the front of the mill, men are erecting the fireworks set pieces for that night's display.

Parading across the companies yard on the corner of Quay and Sea Streets is the Whitbread's lorry trade entry to Newport Carnival. The flat bed of the lorry is bedecked with hops and vines with the girls advertising the various beers produced by the firm.

Making its way up Newport High Street from the Quay Street assembly area is one of the horse drawn carnival floats. Large crowds lined the streets around the town for this very popular spectacle and to admire the enormous amount of hard work that had been put into the exhibits.

The Fordson tractor with trailer in tow has pulled up outside Wadham's and The Red Lion public house in St James's Square to let the passengers on the float greet the Carnival King and Queen who were stood with the mayor on the dais. The tractor's exhaust has been lengthened to make it look like a steam engine and also to take the fumes away from the passengers.

In Lugley Street just up from The Sun Inn on the corner of Holyrood Street in August 192? before the start of the carnival, is the trade entry of Frank Cheverton. The Fordson tractor displaying the fact that it could do the work of the six horses on road or farm. There is also sign advertising BP Oil and Shell Tractor Oil.

It was not until recent times that shops opened all day on a Thursday. Therefore, Thursday afternoon was the half day when social functions and events could be guaranteed to take place. From Newport football ground looking towards the cattle market with Westmore's the hauliers roof shown on the left are the Judges and Committee of the Newport Dog Club posing for the camera prior to the show taking place later in the day.

The ground in Church Litten is in this photograph of the 1903-4 Newport Football Club team. The lads wearing the IWFA badge were also representatives of the county. The snake buckle belts and the boots are long gone. The young man sitting behind the ball was the Captain, E.B. Fewnham, and behind him stands G. Yelf; the remaining players are unknown.

The ground at Church Litten held cup finals for several years before this particular one. It shows a good crown of locals, soldiers and two police officers watching the presentation of the Douglas Hall Cup and medals to the winning Freshwater Royal Garrison Artillery Battalion [RGA] team who had beaten Ryde on Saturday the 19 April 1913. The silverware was presented by the Revd Charles Collis MA, the vicar of St Paul's, Barton Village.

This photograph in the road outside The Clarendon Arms in Clarendon Street is from around 1930. At that time Albert Pointer was the landlord. The Bowls Team from the Castle Bowling Green, which was at the top of Castle Road on the north side, are also shown here. The bowling green was privately owned by Mr William Blake who lived quite conveniently next door.

CRICKET GROUND, VICTORIA ROAD, NEWPORT, I.O.W.   H. 115

Opened in 1901, the Victoria Recreational Ground was also the home of Newport Cricket Club. This photograph from around 1950 shows a very good crowd sat all around the out field watching play. The amount of spectators probably means that this was a Thursday afternoon trades game.

This photograph shows what is believed to be a visiting touring side in front of the pavilion at the Victoria Recreational Ground at Newport, around 1930. The fascia of the building has not changed over the one hundred years since it was erected.

A view of the Newport Rowing Club Boathouse from the 1920s looks down the River Medina towards the Folly Reach. The club was formed in 1863 and over the years the clubhouse which started as a small shed had been extended with decks, clubroom and slipway. Still going strong members of the club are very active in encouraging local youngsters to get involved with the sport

Newport Rowing Club Regatta was a yearly event held on the river in late summer. This view shows a rowing boat from around 1920 bearing King Neptune and his entourage. The rowing boat is dressed with a canopy and various coloured glass night lights can be seen hanging from wires stretched towards the stern. In the background can be seen other vessels taking part in the regatta.

King Neptune with his seaweed covered minions stand in the entrance to the Rowing Club boathouse. After the regatta finished members would adjourn to The Ship and Launch public house, a stone's throw away downstream, to continue their revelry under the watchful eye of Mrs Sheaf the licensee.

The swimming pool at Seaclose is now gone and has been replaced by council offices. Built in 1936 the pool was used by the many schools in the Newport area for swimming lessons in the summer term enabling over the years many thousands of children to obtain their various triangular badges. Although the water was always cold, it was better than school lessons.

Looking at the dress of the young lady riders and the spectators, would suggest a date of around the late 1920s for this photograph of a gymkhana in Nine Acres field, Newport. Elm Grove is in the background with The Gardeners Rest on the right hand side.

With their back to South View the mayor and corporation have turned out in force in Nine Acres field for the opening of an agricultural show around 1920. The shows took place here before moving onto the site at Blackwater Road which gave more room for displays and exhibitions and later enabled the school to be built on the Nine Acres site.

A. Stevens the Cowes photographer's image from around 1920 at Nine Acres field shows cattle which were entered into the agricultural show.

Morey's wood yard chimney is in the background as well as South View. This pre-First World War photograph from the agricultural show at Nine Acres field is a good advertisement for Wood's of Pyle Street, Newport, agricultural implement suppliers and ironmongers whose business must have been good judging by the amount of 'sold' signs.

The man with the straw boater on his head sits inadvertently hiding the advertisement for the Royal Isle of Wight Agricultural Show Ploughing Match in the summer of 1908. The horses and single-handed plough are being readied for the event which was fiercely contested by the island farms.

Nine Acres field off Trafalgar Road was used not only for shows, sports and Gymkhana's but also by the members of the Isle of Wight Motorcycle Club to show off their skills with their machines including a game of hockey no doubt giving great delight to the audience. It looks a robust game with not only motorcycles coming into close contact but also hockey sticks flying through the air.

Seven

From Four Legs to Four Wheels

Mr Harry Webber sits with his dog and passenger in the driving seat of his horse and cart at the rear of his premises at No. 94 High Street, Newport around 1920. He was one of a number of fruiterers and florists in the High Street and was in business from the 1890s to the 1930s. It was not unknown for him and his staff to be working all night making up wreaths for the funerals on the following day. His shop has changed names many times since then and was of late occupied by Happy Daze a record shop.

Newport Railway Station is shown here looking towards the town. The engine with five carriages in tow is a Brighton Class built in the late 1800s and brought over to the island in 1902. The engine driver and fireman are on board the foot plate as is another person. The train is heading on the five mile journey to Cowes.

There is very little that can be said of this Royal Horse Artillery Soldier who was photographed around 1910 in Trafalgar Lane behind Node Hill. He would have been billeted at Albany Barracks but was probably a local man. The soldier and his mount are about halfway along the lane looking towards Chapel Street and above his head is an advertising sign for 'Joinery, Carpentry and Upholstery' which was no doubt at the rear of A.E. King's premises in Node Hill.

An immaculate open-topped motor car, shown here just prior to the First World War, is stood in the old Newport Football Club ground at Church Litten, towards the back entrance where the fairs and circuses were sited. Pan Mills chimney can be seen smoking away in a southerly breeze and to the left is Pan Mill cottage. The fields in the distance now contain the houses of Staplers and Pan Estate. A mill has stood in some form at this site on the River Medina since the fourteenth century, although it has been rebuilt and enlarged many times since. John Thomas was the owner of Pan Mill at the time of this photograph and he was also a partner of Mr Ash at Blackwater Mill, two miles further upstream.

Standing proudly alongside his horse and cart outside of Westmore's in Church Litten around 1920 is Harry Knight of No. 4 Barton Road, Newport known locally as Bantam. Born in Newport in 1876, on leaving school Harry worked for Edward Morris in the High Street delivering hardware with their horse-drawn cart. On buying his own outfit which he stabled alongside The Rowbarge Inn, in Pyle Street he took on contract work picking up the early daily newspapers at Newport station and delivering them to Greengrass's in the High Street seven days a week.

Harry Knight is seen here outside his daughter Ethel's house in Collingwood Road, Newport. Bantam was so proud of his outfit he constantly polished the brasses and blackened the harnesses to make them gleam to make it the best looking team in Newport. His other work was for Eastman the butcher delivering meat to Camphill Prison three days a week, also carting crates of 'pop' for Gould Hibbard and Randall at Church Litten. When work was short he would be waiting outside of sales and was ready and able to load and deliver customers' purchases. Harry Knight continued using horse drawn carts until he retired.

This photograph from 1906 shows DL77, one of the four double-decker buses a year after they were initially brought over to the island and put into service by the Isle of Wight Motor Express Syndicate. You can see passengers waiting on the bus outside The Rose & Crown public house in St Thomas's Square. The buses were unsuccessful and later that year due to bad road conditions, under-powered engines and lack of support they were returned to the mainland. By the door of the pub can be seen a notice board advertising books of tickets and half-price fares. The Rose and Crown building has stood on this site since the 1600s and probably with a different name long before that. These were exceptionally busy premises, especially when the square was used as a corn market and also as a base, or terminus, for the carters and carriers who plied their trade outside. The brick building next door, known as the Charter House, was owned by J. Gould who was originally a grocer, baker and provisions merchant; but best known as an aerated water manufacturer and brewer of the famous 'Carisbrooke' ginger beer. The firm started in the early 1870s and later, in the 1930s, moved to much larger premises at the far end of Church Litten, after amalgamating with the firm of Hibberd from Ventnor and Randall from Ryde and continued to make soft drinks until being taken over by the Beecham Corp. The entire square was occupied for six days a week by the carriers with their carts and vans parked here. Their horses were stabled nearby. A special service was offered by the carriers delivering goods to your doorstep; which was ideal in the many rural areas as the omnibus services did not extend to here.

The popularity of motorcycles had increased at an astonishing rate during the first quarter of the century. Much cheaper to buy and run than the motor car, they became a good means of transport on the island roads. It was then inevitable that a motorcycle club should be formed as this photograph shows. The Isle of Wight Motorcycle Club had its inaugural run on Tuesday 4 May 1920.

The meeting took place in Drill Hall Road, Newport outside of the Drill Hall on a fine and sunny day. Over twenty-five motorcycles and motorcycle combinations paraded before the run.

The motorcycle and outfits drew a good crowd of onlookers, as this must have been quite a curiosity at that time. Behind the display of bikes with their rigid frames and acetylene lamps is the chimney of Westminster Mill looming upwards and to the left hand side is the terrace of three storey houses, whose Victorian ground floor canopies are now long gone. The marks left by this covering structure, however, can still be seen today.

The two men on their machines at the front were the marshals of the run. Both machines are Isle of Wight-registered; DL805 was a Side Valve Zenith.

The Isle of Wight Motorcycle Club members are displaying their bikes outside of the south entrance to the church in St Thomas's Square around 1920. Flat caps and goggles were the order of the day. In the background is Mr Bowler's pawnbrokers shop his sign displayed between the third floor windows.

The natural progression from riding a motorcycle for pleasure is to take it on the racing circuit or dirt track. Here seen in the early 1920s on St George's Down riding between the trials sections is a DL registered machine, being ridden by a smiling chap wearing a trilby hat.

The same location but with a different machine and rider again a local registration but it has not been possible to determine the make. The rider has not removed the acetylene lamp on the handlebars before taking off to the sections.

This photograph from around 1920 shows three smiling employees of J. Warder. The lorry was chain driven with no front doors and had acetylene lamps and is locally registered as DL3707. The vehicle was later taken over by E.J. Hayles contractor of Godshill.

Taken in the early 1930s DL4614 also belonged to James Warder whose offices were towards the bottom of Pyle Street at No. 136. He was a local haulage contractor moving anything from sand and gravel to cattle and sheep for farmers. This view was taken in Collingwood Road, Newport on the south side with Nelson Road visible in the background.

Pyle Street at its junction with St James's Square shows the 15A Southern Vectis single-decker bus serving the Whitepit Lane area approaching the terminus. Not much has changed on the buildings' fascias, just a few owners names.

The winter of 1929 brought several inches of snow to Newport as seen here on Horsebridge Hill outside the chapel just south of Noke Common Road junction. The single-decked ADC 416 bus making for Newport has the registration number DL5578 just visible.

These four gents seated in the Isle of Wight registered opened topped tourer are located either at the rear of the old police station in Fairlee Road or in the gas works. The railway viaduct leading off to Ryde can be seen to the right as can the Whitbread's store and offices which were situated at Quay Street's junction with Sea Street. St Thomas's church tower can be made out in the distance.

It is thought that one of the two men standing by the Pratts Spirit delivery lorry is Peter Hodges, the driver's mate, standing on the right. South Street at the junction with Church Litten from around 1925 shows The Prince of Wales public house on the corner of Town Lane. To the right is the grocery and general shop owned by Mrs Thomas Carwarding which is now Tomlinson's the florist. The Prince of Wales has been in existence since the 1870s and was a typical beer house but shortly after the time of this photograph the owners, the local brewer Mew Langton, decided to alter the exterior into the mock Tudor style as many of the island pubs had already been transformed in this manner. In the background can be seen the sign board for the premises of Fred Salter who was a van and cart builder, a wheelwright and general smith. Mr Salter had been trading in South Street since the early 1900s and made a very good living from the carters who were using the stabling behind him in Tontines Yard and St Thomas' Square. By 1930 the firm had gone.

Eight
Shide Submerged

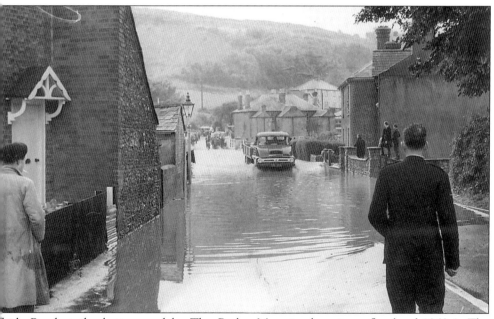

Shide Road at the bottom end by The Barley Mow in the winter floods of 1960-1. The torrential rain in conjunction with adverse spring tides held the excess water back causing flooding both along the River Medina here at Shide and the Lukely Stream at Carisbrooke and Newport. Here a Thames Trader lorry is battling its way through the flood towards dry land.

Looking down from Medina Avenue into Shide Path, residents Mrs Toogood and Mrs Hayle
followed by Brian Toogood and Nip Hayles are making for dry land after their bungalows ha
been flooded. In the far distance where the water is coming down Shide Path in a torrent i
Albert Hart standing in about 2ft of water. The beer store at The Barley Mow public house a
the far end of Shide Path was flooded and the stock of bottles and wooden beer kegs, all full
were washed down the path with the majority of the stock ending up in the swollen Rive
Medina heading towards Newport.

94

The River Medina to the south of Shide Bridge overflowed and submerged the old railway line as well as the lower part of the field which now sells the Christmas trees each December opposite The Barley Mow. The disused railway station can be seen in the centre of the photograph along with Bridge Cottage and the houses on the lower side of Blackwater Road, all now long gone. The beef cattle do not seem to be bothered by the water taking over their field. After the flood eventually receded, the damage to the homes and businesses had to be assessed and repaired. The hardest thing to remove was the mud slurry which washed into the premises with the water. After the first flood on 1 October 1960 the premises were still in the process of drying out when the flooding occurred again the following February, causing the same problems. The Mayor of Newport set up a flood relief fund for those affected and money poured in not just from the local population but also from the mainland. Eventually the Medina and Lukely Rivers were widened and straightened which solved the problem.

From the end of the platform at Shide Station, this photograph is looking in the direction of Newport, showing the flooded track or what was left of it and the natural course of the river bearing under the bridge and off to the left. Tons of gravel from the railway track bed were swept into the gardens of the bungalows in Shide Path which caused problems removing it.

Even though much of the low lying areas around Newport were under water work had to go on and deliveries were still to be made. This photograph from 1 October 1960 is of a Bedford lorry belonging to Island Transport making its way along flooded Sea Street towards the Quay Street.

ea Street again, this time with a view of a timber delivery lorry belonging to H.W. Morey of West Street, Newport fording the flood water with their competitors Alex Sharp and Co.'s remises in the background under several feet of water.

The same flood but a different location, this time at Coppins Bridge. The bus in the background is stuck on the bridge with water in front and also behind in Barton Road. The Prince Regent public house, the chemist's, Ken Harbours electrical shop as well as Mr Messenger's newsagents and a private dwelling can all be seen under several feet of water. The railway viaduct remains which had not yet been demolished can be seen in the background.

This view is on the right hand side at the bottom of the High Street at Coppins Bridge. It shows the flood water in the grocers, the tobacconists and G. Nevison the butcher's shop, all of these premises were family owned businesses and are now all gone.

Nine

The Road to Blackwater

SHIDE BRIDGE IN THE 17TH CENTURY.

This image is taken from an aquatint engraving by Charles Tomkins found in his book *Tour to the Isle of Wight*, 1793. In this view of Shide Bridge and Bridge Cottage the track disappears up and over St George's Down towards Arreton.

The bottom of South Mall, St John's Road around 1906, shows the mall with its protective railings which are still in place today but the pavement on the west side is just hard-core. There is very little motor traffic at this time just delivery horses and carts. The Board School and Technical School are in the distance.

South Mall, this time the top end looking into Newport at the junction with Cypress Road. Across the road are raised cobbles left over from the Victorian era. These cobbles were put in place to enable ladies to keep their shoes and long dresses clean when crossing from pavement to pavement, without them dragging through the muddy surface. The stationary van registration number TH7847 belongs to the Lyons tea and cocoa wholesaler.

Clarence Road around 1920 looking up towards Mount Pleasant Road. York House on the corner of York Road to the right, filling the picture, was the home of the surgeon and physician George Raymond. The house later became a nursing home for expectant mothers which was run by Mrs Meech; who had previously been a sister at Whitecroft Hospital.

The delivery lad with his basket turns up in street scenes wherever a photographer appeared! This pre-1910 photograph is from the top of Clarence Road, and is looking down towards Medina Avenue and the now demolished Oyster Shell Cottages. In the 1840s these cottages were known as Wood's Terrace but why they changed is not known to the author.

1948. Cypress Road, Newport, I.O.W.

Cypress Road around 1920 at its junction with Mount Pleasant Road. Not a parked car in sight just a lonely motorcycle and sidecar with a DL registration. The houses on the hill were good middle class houses, the occupiers being local doctors, solicitors, veterinary surgeons and business proprietors. Pan Fields and Staplers can be seen away in the distance.

Although this photograph is captioned Shide Path, which it was, we know it now as Medina Avenue. The photographer of this image, from around 1930, must have been standing in the road where the new flats have since been built at the rear of Marks and Spencer's. To the right houses are being constructed towards the exclusive Brethren Meeting Room on the corner of Clarence Road. To the left are the Oyster Shell Cottages and behind the hedge is what was to become Matthew's Wood Yard.

This photograph of Avondale Road, by F.N. Broderick in 1910, is looking up from Shide Path. The road has hardly changed in nearly a century, the size and style of the houses hardly altered at all.

This view of Medina Avenue from its junction with Cypress Road and looking towards Newport. A gas lamp can be seen outside what was the grocery shop owned by Mr Stevens he was a very smart and courteous man who, with only one leg, used a crutch to nip around his small shop. These little shops had an atmosphere and smell all of their own.

In the middle-ground is the Railway Spur Line leading to Shide Chalk Pit and into Shide Watermill in the centre of the photograph. The field in the foreground now contains bungalows and gardens in Shide Path. The chimney to the left of the mill was to exhaust the fumes from the gas engine which assisted with powering the grinding wheel.

Shide Watermill and Shide Path in the snow early in 1926. In the field at the bottom of the path where the footbridge runs over the River Medina are chicken houses belonging to Mr Ransom who owned Shide grocery and post office at the top of Shide Path. The shop is still there and has changed hand several times and is now owned by Roger Buttery and his wife June.

Shide Station around 1930 with a light covering of snow on the platform. This line was shut down in 1952 under the Dr Beeching Plan. To the left is Bridge Cottage and to the right is the Barley Mow end of Shide Path.

Looking at Shide Station from the Blackwater direction showing the station master's house and a train waiting at the platform, around 1920. The train has a destination board for Ventnor Town on its smoke stack. The original Barley Mow public house and Shide Golf Club hut is to the left.

Shide Station around 1905 with a family group posing for the photographer complete with a splendid perambulator and canopy – also the obligatory delivery boy standing behind mother and child! There are locally found lumps of chalk surrounding the platform garden beneath the Isle of Wight Central Railway notice board. There had been a station at Shide since 1875 when the railway line was opened between there and Sandown. The final mile was finished about four years later allowing the village to be linked to the main Newport Station with the through connections there. Except for its first four years it was never an extremely busy station but it was needed as the main road passed over the railway lines and had to be guarded by the level crossing gates which necessitated a Station Master. A public house or beer house has stood in Shide for over 150 years and like many others belonging to Mews was transformed into the mock Tudor style in the 1930s. The golf club hut which sat on the pub car park eventually made its way up onto St George's Down when the course was enlarged towards Arreton and the Chalk Pit extended.

At the bottom of the lane on the right is the track leading to Shide Dairy. This photograph looks towards the houses of the corner of Blackwater Road with St George's Down and Pan Chalk Pit in the distance.

Shide Road at its junction with Blackwater Road and St George's Lane, showing houses on the left which were demolished prior to the river widening scheme and long before the building of the new road. The house in the centre of the picture with the bay window is No. 70 Shide Road which at the time of this photograph (around 1910) was a little front room sweet shop, which remained until after the Second World War.

A detachment of militia from Albany Barracks are seen making their way up Burnt House Lane from Pan Lane. It is believed that they were in search of a escapee from an outside working party from Parkhurst Prison.

Shide Bridge on the corner of Blackwater Road with Bridge Cottage and the station master' house to the right. The level crossing gates are shut. This photograph is from around 192(before the road was tarmacked.

Photographed half way along Blackwater Road, near the bottom of Conker Avenue are a gang of Cheek's road workers laying the kerb line under the bank. This picture is from the late 1920s.

In February 1911, the Isle of Wight Fox Hounds met at Blackwater House the home of Mrs Pearce, before setting off across the countryside. These meets were quite a spectacle with followers travelling long distances on foot to attend. The hounds at this time were kept at Marvel.

This remarkable, although somewhat faded photograph, is of Mr William Orchard standing in his blacksmiths forge at Blackwater in 1919 after he took over the premises from Mr Mansbridge his first employer, with whom he started his apprenticeship in around 1890. Mr Orchard worked for various blacksmiths still learning the trade including Mr Hawkins of Hunnyhill and Mr Walter Prince of Sea Street, Newport. On his first retirement at the age of seventy-two in 1947 Mr William Orchard's son Charles took over the management of the business with Mr Orchard Sr 'lending a hand if needed'. However in the mid-1950s Mr Orchard Jr had to give up shoeing horses so his father returned to the forge, staying on until his second retirement at the grand age of eighty-five. The sub-post office next door to the forge was run by Mr Orchard's wife Bertha who was still serving her customers at the age of eighty-four.

Ten

Carisbrooke and District

Carisbrooke Mill or Kents Mill as it was also known from an engraving by Bingley around 1840, had been in existence since the 1300s and was one of the main watermills on the island with its pond stretching back nearly as far as Clatterford Shute. Its working life ended just before the outbreak of war in 1939 and is now privately owned.

The road from Newport High Street to Carisbrooke starts here. This photograph from around 1905 shows the shops at the top of the town with the blinds shielding the goods in the windows from the sun. The shop at the front on the right is Wray's the bakers and confectioners.

The buildings on Alexandra Terrace at the start of Carisbrooke Road were the most elegantly designed and built three storey town houses in Newport. The properties have either a balcony or bay window on the first floor looking out onto the wide mall and main road.

This photograph from around 1910 looks a little further up the mall towards the town centre with Portland Street leading off to the right. All the children in the scene are wearing leather boots with the boys in breeches and caps.

Looking down at a snow covered Cedar Hill on 30 December 1908. This plate photograph was published as a Christmas postcard the following year and was posted on Christmas Day morning in Newport and delivered locally later that day. The heavily snow laden boughs of the cedar trees in the grounds of Beechwood are making a canopy above the roadway helping to make a spectacular scene.

Taken by the Ryde photographer F.N. Broderick around 1905, the shepherd is standing with his flock of black-faced sheep half-way up Cedar Hill, probably making their way towards Whitcombe. At the bottom of the hill can just be made out a box wagon loaded with sacks outside of Mr Sanders, the market gardeners premises. Out of sight in this picture and opposite Mr Sanders' home, stood a beer house called The Three Blackbirds. This is now long gone and has been replaced by a row of terrace cottages. It was, like so many at that time, a den of iniquity with smuggled goods being stored and sold on the premises with the inn keeper always one step ahead of the excise men. Cedar Hill before Castle Road and Whitepit Lane were built, was used as the main road to Carisbrooke Castle for vehicles because they did not have to ford a stream as in Spring Lane and Castle Street.

From 12 May 1937, this overhead triumphal arch displayed over Recreation Ground Road, was for the Coronation that day of King George VI and Queen Elizabeth. Celebrations took place on the Victoria Ground during the day.

The Eight Bells pond and boating lake with the bowling green behind looking towards Carisbrooke church around 1910. A tranquil scene with cows grazing in what are now the gardens of the houses in Castle Hill.

The author was reliably informed that the vehicle in this photograph is a 1907 Vauxhall, registration number DL341. The man in the passenger's seat was Mr R. Gallop who was instructing a pupil to drive in The Eight Bell yard in Carisbrooke High Street.

Looking up Carisbrooke High Street are the long gone terrace of houses on the left. Cooke and Burt were the butchers on the right and Bertha Campbell was the licensee of The Castle Hotel selling Dashwoods Carisbrooke Ales at the time of this photograph around 1905.

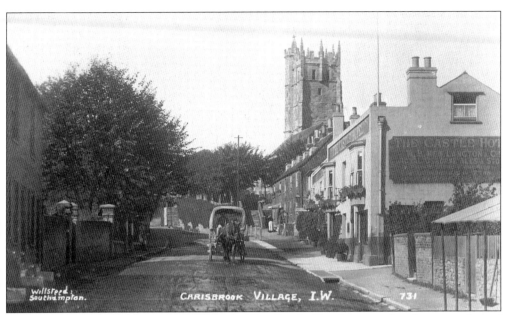

When photographed here in around 1910, The Castle Hotel was under the ownership of W.B. Mew, Langton and Co. and looks a lot tidier than it did in the previous photograph. Accommodation is still offered to travellers and no doubt it traded on its name with visitors to the near by Carisbrooke Castle.

This good photographic postcard shows a coach and four in hand in front of The Red Lion Hotel in Carisbrooke High Street around 1913.

You could not have found a more marvellous situation for a gang of pipe layers to take a rest from their hard labour at this convenient stop outside of The Red Lion public house in Carisbrooke High Street in around 1920.

A pleasant view from outside what is now the newsagents in Carisbrooke High Street looking down at the horses and carriages pulled up outside of the church hall on a sunny day in the summer of 1905.

Two young children sit on the steps below the gas lamp that leads up to St Mary's churchyard, Carisbrooke, around 1907. The steps nearly one hundred years ago were exceptionally worn due to their continued use over the previous centuries.

A village scene around 1920 with a woman and two children stood with their backs to Attrill's bakery and shop in the High Street, probably waiting for a Colsons bus to take them to Newport.

"GLENFIELD"
CARISBROOKE.

The Beauty Spot of the Island.

Private Hotel & Boarding House

Stands in its own beautiful Grounds,
adjoining Carisbrooke Castle. Well
appointed and comfortable Dining and
Drawing Rooms. Lounge. An Ideal
Centre for Visitors who wish "to do
the Island."

———

Parties catered for.
Luncheons and Teas served in Glenfield Grounds.

TELEPHONE: MISSES CAVE, *Proprietresses*
NEWPORT 2660.

An advertising card from the 1930s for the
Glenfield Private Hotel and Boarding
House which was situated on Cemetery Hill
known now as Whitcombe Road just up
from the junction with Cedar Hill.

This photograph is from St Mary's church steps, around 1910, shows Mount Joy and the
cemetery on the hill in the distance. The long gone terrace of houses with their chalk whitened
front steps can also be seen in the centre of the picture. Two road sweepers can also be seen in
the distance near to The Eight Bells public house.

120

As the caption describes Glenholme is the first house under Carisbrooke Castle and is situated in Millers Lane. The owner Mrs Denham is stood with her daughter outside of the front door. Refreshments were offered in the tea garden and plain tea was just 6d. The premises were ideally situated at the bottom of the footpath just below the castle entrance.

The ford at the bottom of Castle Street is shown with the keep of Carisbrooke Castle in the distance. Springvale offered visitors to the village not only teas in the garden but also overnight accommodation.

Time for a quick rest and cooling drink in Castle Street ford for the pair of horses drawing the milkcart.

Tea gardens were in vogue in Castle Street in 1906 the time of this photograph. The passing trade would have been pedestrian making the offer of refreshments quite a viable pursuit for the householders with gardens.

122

From the field just below the castle entrance around 1910 Carisbrooke Mill with its outbuildings can be seen. The tea gardens in Millers Lane is at the bottom of the picture, and the thatched cottage with the two chimneys was the home of the donkey keeper at the castle.

A perfect view looking down towards Clatterford Shute and the Bowcombe Valley showing Clatterford House which was owned by George A. Brannon who was a descendant of the Victorian engraver and printer. The Brannon family were the publishers of the successful Isle of Wight County Press.

THE I.W. FOX HOUNDS MEET AT CARISBROOKE CASTLE, JAN. 1907.

The Isle of Wight Fox Hounds are shown here meeting at Carisbrooke Castle in 1907. It was always a very well attended event judging by the amount of spectators all dressed in their Sunday best.

The following three photographs are all from 30 December 1908 by the Southampton photographer Mr Willsteed. Millers Lane looks spectacular with the snow on the thatched roofs and Carisbrooke church tower is visible in the distance.

Lovers Walk or The Shrubbery as it is now known looks extremely pretty under a good covering of snow. This view is looking down towards Spring Lane.

Quite a few inches of snow lay on the footpath and hedges leading from the southwest corner of Carisbrooke Castle walls up towards the junction with Whitcombe Road and the lane to Froglands.

It is rare to find photographs of rural Wight at the best of times but this one is of the Isle of Wight Fox Hounds meeting on Thursday 28 March 1907 at Walnut Tree Green, Bowcombe. Was the police officer from Newport Borough, there for traffic or crowd control?

Walnut Tree Green, Bowcombe again on the same day in March. More Bowcombe residents are in this photograph who no doubt are waiting to follow the hunt up over Bowcombe Down in the background.

The Fox Hounds met at Park Cross, Carisbrooke in this photograph, which is the grassy island on the Calbourne Road at its junction with Betty Haunt Lane. The Blacksmiths Arms public house can be seen on the hill in the background.

The Isle of Wight Fox Hounds would meet all over the island to hunt but on Friday 11 March 1910 Park Cross, Carisbrooke was the assembly area. As this event took place in the week, it was normally only those involved who would follow the hounds. The women in the photograph would have followed, either in the chauffeur driven open topped touring car, or the horse and buggy seen behind, using the lanes and roads to view the chase.

The gents photographed outside The Blacksmiths Arms public house or Betty Aunt as it was locally known were all in Sunday best, and probably on their way to Newport. Looking at the stones under the wheels, the wagon would have had poor brakes so Alvington Shute must have been an exciting ride. The landlord of the public house at this time in 1906 was James Edward Cooper which was a very common name in the licensing trade on the Isle of Wight. There had been some form of inn at Park Cross, Carisbrooke since early in the 1700s when the original building was a blacksmith's forge with a beer serving room within, hence the name of the premises. The nearby Betty Haunt Lane, by which The Blacksmiths Arms is known locally probably derives its name from a landlady of the inn or a lady from a nearby house who was murdered in the lane. The building, like many of the licensed premises on the island in bygone days have had smuggling connections with illicit goods being stored within the building or nearby. With its unique location and expansive views the excise men could easily be spotted from afar.